THE SIX CHAPLET
ROSARY

ST PAULS

Cover illustrations by Maurizio Boscolo
By courtesy of Edizioni San Paolo srl, Cinisello Balsamo (Milano), Italy

ST PAULS
Middlegreen, Slough SL3 6BT, United Kingdom
Moyglare Road, Maynooth, Co. Kildare, Ireland

© ST PAULS (UK) 1994

ISBN 085439 473 7

Typesetting by TuKan, High Wycombe
Printed by Società San Paolo, Rome

ST PAULS is an activity of the priests and brothers of the Society of St Paul who proclaim the Gospel through the media of social communication

The Six Chaplet Rosary

The Opening Mysteries

Creation
The call of Abraham
God's covenant with Moses
The Birth of Samuel
God's covenant with David

The Prophetic Mysteries

Elijah: Sign of the coming day of the Lord
The Immanuel prophecy of Isaiah
The Suffering Servant prophecy
The son of man prophecy
John the Baptist, the forerunner

The Joyful Mysteries

The Annunciation
The Visitation
The Nativity
The Presentation
The Finding in the temple

The Sorrowful Mysteries

The Agony in th garden
The Scourging
The Crowning with thorns
Carrying the cross
Crucifixion

The Glorious Mysteries

The Resurrection
The Ascension
The Descent of the Holy Spirit
The Dormition/Assumption of the
Blessed Virgin Mary
The Crowning of the Blessed Virgin Mary

The Continuing Mysteries

The Saints
The Martyrs
The Angels and Archangels
Christ the great High Priest in Heaven
The Second Coming

Introduction

The traditional three chaplet rosary has been in use for many centuries. However, though the mysteries of the rosary are wonderful in helping the devotee to grow more deeply into the Christian faith, there seem to be other mysteries which could well be introduced into an enlarged rosary. The six chaplet rosary does incorporate the traditional rosary. However, as the name suggests, three other categories of mystery are added to the traditional ones. These are: the Opening Mysteries, the Prophetic Mysteries and the Continuing Mysteries. The first two precede the traditional rosary and the last one follows afterwards. It is hoped that meditation on these additional mysteries will further help to deepen human understanding of the divine revelation.

In this presentation of the rosary there is a pattern for each of the mysteries. An appropriate biblical passage is used in each case, followed by a prayer. Those who wish to add intercessions will naturally create their own additional material. However, some suggestions for further thought and meditation are given with each of the mysteries.

If the intention behind using the rosary is to penetrate more deeply into the revealed mysteries of the faith, it is surely more helpful to take time for prayer and meditation rather than to rush through the rosary. Certainly, in the six chaplet rosary it is the intention that the user should have ample space to extend his or her thoughts.

◆

Introductory prayer

O God, I dedicate this rosary
to the Blessed Virgin Mary
and I give thanks for her work
as the Mother of Jesus.
I give thanks also for the pure love
of Mary's parents, Joachim and Anne.
For the Presentation of Mary in the Temple,
I thank you, Lord;
and for all the love that comes to us
through the Holy Family I praise you.
Guide my prayers and meditations
during my recital of this rosary. Amen.

THE FIRST CHAPLET:

The Opening Mysteries

1. Creation

In the beginning God created the heavens and the earth. The earth was without form and void, and darkness was upon the face of the deep; and the Spirit of God was moving over the face of the waters.

Genesis 1:1-2

Prayer

O God, I worship you and adore you, enthroned as you are in the majesty and glory of your creative power. Help me to understand more deeply the mysteries of your creation. I know through this body and mind that you have given me that the universe is vast and unimaginable. Yet even the whole of creation is but a single strand in the tapestry of your thought. I love the sky, and the oceans and the mountains. I stand in time and space, and wonder at the beauty of the flowers and at the variety of life forms which you have made. I ponder on the nature of heaven, also your creation, and I thank you that you have prepared another place for us to delight in after the wonders of this life have passed away. O

God, Father, Son, and Holy Spirit, I praise you for the mystery of creation. Amen.

Themes for meditation

The miracle of the five senses.
The creative gifts that God has given to
    human beings.
God's ultimate purpose in creating people.
Opportunities to cooperate with our Creator in
    the learning process of this life.
What opportunities can I create for other
    people?

◆

Our Father . Hail Mary . Glory be to the Father

2. The call of Abraham

Now the Lord said to Abram, "Go from your country and your father's house to the land that I will show you. And I will make of you a great nation, and I will bless you and make your name great, so that you will be a blessing"

Genesis 12:1-2

Prayer

O God, thousands of years ago you spoke to Abraham and made him a wonderful promise which was fulfilled in the Jewish nation to which Jesus belonged; and which has also been fulfilled spiritually in the Christian Church. I thank you for revealing your purposes to Abraham and I pray that you will help me to understand more deeply the nature of your revelation through the Scriptures and the Church. I give thanks also for all those other men and women who have heard your call and have obeyed your voice. Help me to understand the nature of your call to me, O Lord, and grant me the grace to be obedient. As you walked with Abraham, so also walk with me through the years of my earthly life and guide me to the promised land where all saints and angels reside with you in love and peace. Amen.

Themes for meditation

God's long term planning.
The nature of God's covenant with humanity.
God's mysterious way of working his will.
People of other faiths.
Childless couples who are longing for a baby.

◆

Our Father . Hail Mary . Glory be to the Father

3. God's covenant with Moses

Then Moses took the book of the covenant, and read it in the hearing of the people; and they said, "All that the Lord has spoken we will do, and we will be obedient." And Moses took the blood and threw it upon the people, and said, "Behold the blood of the covenant which the Lord has made with you in accordance with all these words."

Exodus 24:7-8

Prayer

O God, help me to appreciate the work that Moses did under the guidance of the Holy Spirit. I know that the law of Moses is your law as you revealed it to him. Help me to understand this law in relation to your gracious forgiveness, through Christ, of human transgressions. Moses is still our teacher, but Christ is always our Redeemer, and in this mystery I desire to live my life close to you. Help me to understand the mystery of your covenant with Moses and the Chosen People. Through blood you blessed that covenant and through the blood of Christ you bless your covenant with the Church of Christ. I thank you for the life and work of Moses and for the prefiguring of the idea of redemption in the release of the Jewish slaves from their bondage in Egypt. So release me from my sins, O God, and guide me through the great wilderness that lies between me and your Promised Land. Amen.

Themes for meditation

The Transfiguration, at which Moses and Elijah were present.
The Ten Commandments.
The sign of the burning bush given to Moses.
God's name as revealed to Moses ["I am who I am"].
Prisoners of conscience today.

◆

Our Father . Hail Mary . Glory be to the Father

4. The Birth of Samuel

"For this child I prayed; and the Lord has granted me my petition which I made to him. Therefore I have lent him to the Lord; as long as he lives, he is lent to the Lord." And they worshipped the Lord there. Hannah also prayed and said, "My heart exults in the Lord; my strength is exalted in the Lord. My mouth derides my enemies, because I rejoice in thy salvation."

1 Samuel 1:27-2:1

Prayer

I give thanks with Hannah for the birth of her son, Samuel, and I thank you also, Lord, for the pattern for the Magnificat which you placed in the mouth of Hannah. Help me to understand the mystery of the boy Samuel's call in the temple when he heard your voice three times. Help me to appreciate the work of Samuel as an inspired prophet and as the great king maker of Israel. I pray, O Lord, for all parents who wish to have children to love and to cherish and ask that as with Hannah their prayer may be answered. I also pray that you will call men and women today to be your servants in the world to fight against the powers of evil. Amen

Themes for meditation

Difficulties that religious and political leaders
   have to face.
How the voice of God speaks in different ways.
The hurt of being childless.
Dedication of one's life to God.
Being a witness for Christ.

◆

Our Father . Hail Mary . Glory be to the Father

5. God's covenant with David

When your days are fulfilled and you lie down with your fathers, I will raise up your offspring after you, who shall come forth from your body, and I will establish his kingdom. He shall build a house for my name, and I will establish the throne of his kingdom for ever. I will be his father, and he shall be my son.

2 Samuel 7:12-13

Prayer

O God, I know that you chose King David as your adopted son, to make a wonderful prophecy of the coming of your only begotten Son, Jesus Christ, into the world. Help me to appreciate the life and work of King David, your servant. Give me strength as you gave King David strength, that I may face the temptations and dangers of each day. Give me the spiritual power to slay the giants of evil and despair. May I praise you with all my heart, Lord, as King David praised you with his inspired psalms. May I, like David, have faith in your guidance and confidence in your help in time of trouble. Give me the kind of compassion that David had and forgive me as you forgave David when he showed weakness and sinned by stealing another man's wife. Help me in my weak humanity to grow towards Christ each day that my mind and soul may be filled with faith, hope and love. Amen.

Themes for meditation

How God sees the good in us, despite the evil.
How words and music by gifted people can help our worship.
The way God calls ordinary people to do great things.
To keep our faith in God in the face of difficulties.
How God used King David in his revelation of his future plans.

◆

Our Father . Hail Mary . Glory be to the Father

THE SECOND CHAPLET:

The Prophetic Mysteries

1. Elijah: Sign of the coming day of the Lord

And he said, "Go forth, and stand upon the mount before the Lord." And behold, the Lord passed by, and a great and strong wind rent the mountains, and broke in pieces the rocks before the Lord, but the Lord was not in the wind; and after the wind an earthquake, but the Lord was not in the earthquake; and after the earthquake a fire, but the Lord was not in the fire; and after the fire a still small voice. And when Elijah heard it, he wrapped his face in his mantle and went out and stood at the entrance to the cave. And behold, there came a voice to him, and said, "What are you doing here, Elijah?"

1 Kings 19:11-13

Prayer

O God of Pentecost, speak to me in the quiet of my soul, as you spoke to the prophet Elijah. When life is full of storms and everything seems to be falling apart, stand beside me on the mountain, O Lord. Help me to understand and appreciate the life and work of the prophet Elijah. As he was able to stand alone against his enemies, so help me, O God, to stand fast in time of trouble. Give me wisdom to see the significance of Elijah as the sign of the coming Messiah. I know that your word came to the prophets, O Lord, and that they spoke that word to the people of their time. I pray that you will call prophets in this generation so that they may impart your word to our people. Speak, Lord, for your servant is listening. Speak to me now, Lord, in the depths of my soul. Amen.

Themes for meditation

The power of evil in the world and the greater
    power for good.
The healing of the sick.
The destructive power of drought and famine.
The free gifts of rain and sunshine to bring
    good crops.
The power rich nations have to change the
    world.

◆

Our Father . Hail Mary . Glory be to the Father

2. The Immanuel prophecy of Isaiah

*Again the Lord spoke to Ahaz, "Ask a sign of the Lord
your God; let it be as deep as Sheol or high as heaven."
But Ahaz said, "I will not ask, and I will not put the
Lord to the test." And he said, "Hear then, O house of
David! Is it too little for you to weary men, that you
weary my God also? Therefore the Lord himself will
give you a sign. Behold, a young woman shall conceive
and bear a son, and shall call his name Immanuel."*

Isaiah 7:10-14

Prayer

O Lord, grant me the vision to understand your
annunciation of the coming of Christ through
the prophet Isaiah. This mystery is wonderful
to meditate upon, Lord, that you should tell
the world about the Incarnation seven hundred
years before it happened. I give thanks for the
life and work of Isaiah the prophet and for your
revelations through his oracles to the world of
his day. Give me the grace also, O God, to hear
your word and to obey it. As Isaiah was fearless
before the potentates of his time, so make me
fearless in promoting your Gospel to those

around me. If you remain beside me, Lord, I will stand. If you walk with me, Lord, I will not stumble, despite the pains and difficulties life can bring. Abide with me, Lord, as you made your abode with Isaiah of old. Amen.

Themes for meditation

Waiting for God's word.
Christ the Prince of Peace.
Jerusalem on earth and in heaven.
The holiness of God (read Isaiah 6:1-9).
Christ, the corner stone of God's building.

◆

Our Father . Hail Mary . Glory be to the Father

3. The Suffering Servant prophecy

He was despised and rejected by men; a man of sorrows, and acquainted with grief; and as one from whom men hide their faces he was despised, and we esteemed him not. Surely he has borne our griefs and carried our sorrows; yet we esteemed him stricken, smitten by God, and afflicted. But he was wounded for our transgressions, he was bruised for our iniquities; upon him was the chastisement that made us whole, and with his stripes we are healed.

Isaiah 53:3-5

Prayer

I thank you, O God, for the true vision of the prophet who saw beforehand the vicarious suffering of Christ. Help me to understand why people have to suffer in so many ways and what the place of suffering is in your dispensation, O Lord. Give me the wisdom to perceive the ways in which the Jewish nation, into which Christ was born, was your Suffering Servant; and how their suffering prefigured the suffering of Jesus upon the cross. I pray for those who have suffering inflicted upon them needlessly and I pray for those who suffer in love on behalf of others. For those who cannot escape suffering, Lord, I ask your special grace that they may feel their suffering to be part of Christ's suffering. I know, Lord, that you are present in suffering and that out of suffering you can produce miracles of love and service. In the little share of suffering that I have to endure, O God, I pray that you will share it with me. Amen.

Themes for meditation

What it means for me to be God's servant.
Poets and theologians who enrich our
thinking.
Groups of people who are suffering at this
time.
How Christ suffered for all nations and
peoples.
The peace of God which passes understanding.

◆

Our Father . Hail Mary . Glory be to the Father

4. The Son of man prophecy

I saw in the night visions, and behold, with the clouds of heaven there came one like a son of man, and he came to the Ancient of Days and was presented before him. And to him was given dominion and glory and kingdom, that all peoples, nations, and languages should serve him; his dominion is an everlasting dominion, which shall not pass away, and his kingdom one that shall not be destroyed.

Daniel 7:13-14

Prayer

Eternal God, centre of being beyond all time and space, I kneel before you and await your word. I thank you for the prophet Daniel and his timeless visions, especially for his vision of God's Son, eternal with the Father and one with the Holy Spirit. For sending Jesus, Son of man and Messiah, I thank you, O Lord, and I pray for a deeper understanding of this mystery and the prophecies concerning it. I pray for those today who are persecuted and like the heroes of Daniel's day have to endure the fiery furnace. Give them and all innocent victims courage to endure, Lord. I ask for wisdom to understand Daniel's vision of the end of the world and I pray that Christ may come again in glory to rule over both earth and heaven. May my prayers and the prayers of your whole Church be joined to the prayers of all saints and angels in praising your holy name. Amen.

Themes for meditation

The holy and glorious Trinity.
Christ the King of the universe.
The signs and wonders of God.
God's eternal Kingdom contrasted with earthly
    kingdoms which pass away.
The communion of saints.

Our Father . Hail Mary . Glory be to the Father

5. John the Baptist, the forerunner

As it is written in Isaiah the prophet, "Behold I send my messenger before thy face, who shall prepare thy way; the voice of one crying in the wilderness: Prepare the way of the Lord, make his paths straight. "
John the baptizer appeared in the wilderness, preaching a baptism of repentance for the forgiveness of sins.

Mark 1:2-4

Prayer

God, our Father, I know that you called John to announce the imminent coming of the Messiah. I pray for an understanding of his life and work, that I may the better perceive the mystery of the Incarnation. I know that Jesus, your Son, accepted baptism from the hand of John; and I thank you for the gift of baptism to the Church. I pray that I may live up to the promises made at my baptism and that I may hear the call to repentance each day of my life. Above all, Lord, I ask that the gift of baptism by your Holy Spirit may remain with me from now until the end of my days upon earth. Guide

me, Lord, in all that I think or speak or do, that
I may be worthy of a place in heaven. Amen.

Themes for meditation

The cleansing of the spirit.
The wilderness of a life without Christ.
The essentials of life.
The words of the baptismal formula: I baptize
    you in the name of the Father, and of the
    Son, and of the Holy Spirit.
My life as a sacrament.

◆

Our Father . Hail Mary . Glory be to the Father

THE THIRD CHAPLET:

The Joyful Mysteries

1. The Annunciation

In the sixth month the angel Gabriel was sent from God to a city of Galilee named Nazareth, to a virgin betrothed to a man whose name was Joseph, of the house of David; and the virgin's name was Mary. And he came to her and said, "Hail, O favoured one, the Lord is with you!" But she was greatly troubled at the saying, and considered in her mind what sort of greeting this might be. And the angel said to her, "Do not be afraid, Mary, for you have found favour with God. And behold, you will conceive in your womb and bear a son, and you shall call his name Jesus."

Luke 1:26-31

Prayer

O gracious Lord of all power and possibility, I praise you for your wonderful word to Mary through the angel Gabriel. I thank you for those angelic messengers who carry your word to your chosen ones and for those watchful angels who guard the children of the true faith. Give me a share of the wonder that Mary experienced when you chose her to be the mother of the Messiah. I also praise you for speaking to Joseph that he might understand the miraculous conception that was to take place. Fill me with the kind of love that you gave to Mary and Joseph, Lord, that I may explore my potential as your child and servant in the world. I listen for your word, Lord, and I ask that you will use me to do your will in whatever way I am able. Through the Blessed Virgin Mary and all the saints I pray for your daily guidance. Amen.

Themes for meditation

What responsibilities has God given to me?
The miracle of a new life.
The way God chooses ordinary people.
Opening myself to God's word.
How can I open doors for other people?

◆

Our Father . Hail Mary . Glory be to the Father

2. The Visitation

In those days Mary arose and went with haste into the hill country, to a city of Judah, and she entered the house of Zechariah and greeted Elizabeth. And when Elizabeth heard the greeting of Mary, the babe leaped in her womb; and Elizabeth was filled with the Holy Spirit and she exclaimed with a loud cry, "Blessed are you among women, and blessed is the fruit of your womb! And why is this granted me, that the mother of my Lord should come to me? For behold, when the voice of your greeting came to my ears, the babe in my womb leaped for joy. And blessed is she who believed that there would be a fulfilment of what was spoken to her from the Lord."

Luke 1:39-45

Prayer

O God, I thank you and praise you for the loving relationship that Mary and Elizabeth had, and for the insight that you gave Elizabeth on the occasion of Mary's visit. I pray for those who at this time are approaching parenthood and I ask that you will give them the kind of joy that Mary and Elizabeth experienced in anticipating their motherhood. I thank you for the blessing Elizabeth gave to Mary and to Mary's growing child, Jesus. I give thanks also for the faith of these two women whom you called, Lord, and who answered your call so willingly. So may I answer your call to me, Lord, and so may I rejoice in your providential care of the world and all your children. Amen.

Themes for meditation

How I can share my joys and sorrows with
  family and friends.
Children who do not have loving parents.
The words of the Magnificat.
The blessings God has given me.
Unhappy or lonely people.

◆

Our Father . Hail Mary . Glory be to the Father

35

3. The Nativity

And Joseph also went up from Galilee, from the city of Nazareth, to Judea, to the city of David, which is called Bethlehem, because he was of the house and lineage of David, to be enrolled with Mary, his betrothed, who was with child. And while they were there, the time came for her to be delivered. And she gave birth to her first-born son and wrapped him in swaddling cloths, and laid him in a manger, because there was no place for them in the inn.

Luke 2:4-7

Prayer

O Lord, help me to understand the importance of the birth of Jesus as the greatest event in human history. I know that on this event the history of the human race is hinged and I pray that all nations and peoples will come to see that this is so. I thank you for the gift of your Son in the Incarnation and I pray for the redemption of the world through the agency of Jesus Christ, now at your right hand in heaven. I give thanks also for the Bible, which tells the story of your revelation and of the beginning of the process of human redemption. I pray that I may be redeemed, O Lord, and that I may grow to fulfil your plan for me. For all babies born today I ask the blessing of your Son, for they are helpless as he was, and like him need the love of a family around them. I pray for the ideal of family life and that Joseph and Mary may forever be our example in the love they gave to your Son. Amen.

Themes for meditation

God incarnate in a human being.
How love can overcome evil.
All the people who have been inspired by the
    life and example of Jesus.
God's second act of creation through Christ.
The glory of God as revealed to the shepherds.

◆

Our Father . Hail Mary . Glory be to the Father

4. The Presentation

*Now there was a man in Jerusalem, whose name was
Simeon, and this man was righteous and devout,
looking for the consolation of Israel, and the Holy
Spirit was upon him. And it had been revealed to him
by the Holy Spirit that he should not see death before
he had seen the Lord's Christ. And inspired by the
Spirit he came into the temple; and when his parents
brought the child Jesus, to do for him according to the
custom of the law, he took him up in his arms and
blessed God and said, "Lord, now lettest thou thy
servant depart in peace, according to thy word; for
mine eyes have seen thy salvation which thou hast
prepared in the presence of all peoples, a light for
revelation to the Gentiles and for glory to thy people
Israel."*

Luke 2:25-32

Prayer

O God, Father of all nations, help me to know
your Son as clearly as Simeon did, that I may
draw more closely to him. Help me to perceive
how the baby Jesus was destined from before
his birth, according to your plan, to be a light

for all peoples. As Simeon was your faithful
servant until he was old, so may I be your servant
for as many years as you have allotted to me. By
your grace, may I know Christ in spirit during
my earthly life. Yet, I long to see Christ before
my eyes and I pray that in the realm of heaven
I may be counted worthy to come face to face
with my Lord. I pray, therefore, that my sins
may be forgiven, and that my heart may be
filled with your love, both in this life and the
next. So may I then be more aware of your holy
and pure Being which burns throughout the
universe. Amen.

Themes for meditation

Christ the light of the world.
The gifts of the Holy Spirit.
God's salvation working through the Church.
What it means to be righteous and devout as
    Simeon was.
The mission of the Church.

◆

Our Father . Hail Mary . Glory be to the Father

5. The Finding in the temple

After three days they found him in the temple, sitting among the teachers, listening to them and asking them questions; and all who heard him were amazed at his understanding and his answers. And when they saw him they were astonished; and his mother said to him, "Son, why have you treated us so? Behold, your father and I have been looking for you anxiously." And he said to them, "How is it that you sought me? Did you not know that I must be in my Father's house?"

Luke 2:46-49

Prayer

Father of all, I ask you to open my mind to understand the teaching of the Scriptures. I thank you that your Son, Jesus, even as a child, had the wisdom to know the truths of heaven. I pray that a measure of that truth may be enshrined in your Church, that those who listen to your voice may find enlightenment in the darkness of this world. I also pray for the wisdom to ask those questions which will help me to find more about your creation and more about the truths of your revelation to humankind. At the same time, help me to remember that Jesus came to earth to show us the nature of your love; and that love needs only sincerity and simplicity of heart to fulfil itself. Give me a heart that longs to be in your house, O Father, that I may come to worship you and serve you more faithfully each day. I ask these things in the name of your Son, Jesus Christ. Amen.

Themes for meditation

How my life has changed and is changing.
The right priorities in life.
What is truth?
How can I improve my knowledge of the
    Christian faith?
What does God require in my worship?

Our Father . Hail Mary . Glory be to the Father

THE FOURTH CHAPLET:

The Sorrowful Mysteries

1. The Agony in the garden

*And they went to a place which was called Gethsemane;
and he said to his disciples, "Sit here while I pray."
And he took with him Peter and James and John, and
began to be greatly distressed and troubled. And he
said to them, "My soul is very sorrowful, even to
death; remain here, and watch." And going a little
farther, he fell on the ground and prayed that, if it
were possible, the hour might pass from him. And he
said, "Abba, Father, all things are possible to thee;
remove this cup from me; yet not what I will, but
what thou wilt." And he came and found them
sleeping, and he said to Peter, "Simon, are you asleep?
Could you not watch one hour? Watch and pray that
you may not enter into temptation; the spirit indeed is
willing, but the flesh is weak."*

Mark 14:32-38

Prayer

O God, I kneel with Christ in Gethsemane and
try to understand his great love and his great
sorrow as he prepared to die upon the cross.
Like the disciples, I cannot watch for long
because my flesh is weak, but I pray for your

strength within me, Lord, so that I may face the trials and temptations of my own life. I thank you that Jesus was subject to human temptations and difficulties, because I know that he will understand my frailty and that he will walk with me when I do not know which way to turn. I know, Lord, that Jesus accepted the bitter cup of ignominious death so that he could serve humankind. I thank you for our Saviour and for his courage and obedience to the will of his Father. So may I obey your will, Lord, and show courage in the face of danger or pain. Amen.

Themes for meditation

Those who have to face difficult decisions.
Times when I have let God down.
How victory can come out of apparent failure.
Those who show moral courage when in pain
   or distress.
Prisoners of conscience.

◆

Our Father . Hail Mary . Glory be to the Father

2. The Scourging

Then Pilate took Jesus and scourged him.

John 19:1

Prayer

O Lord, I know that you suffered pain and degradation at the hands of cruel men. The hot lash cut into your sacred flesh and those watching laughed scornfully and enjoyed the spectacle. Help me to understand, Lord, why you allowed this to happen, when you are the Lord of all that is and ever was, and ever will be. I pray for those today who have to suffer torture and, though I know they are already in your loving care, I ask that you will come to them as the tortured Christ so that they will know that you are with them in their time of trial. I pray for those in authority in the different countries on our planet and I ask that the spirit of compassion will move them when it is timely; and for those who inflict pain on others, Lord, I ask that they will somehow be brought to understand that they are hurting you as well as their victims, and I pray that they will repent and make amendment for the hurt they have caused. Amen.

Themes for meditation

Why God allows humans and other creatures
    to suffer pain.
The temptation to misuse power.
How God's grace may bring good out of
    suffering.
How Jesus stood alone against evil powers.
How to help victims of crime.

◆

Our Father . Hail Mary . Glory be to the Father

3. The Crowning with thorns

And the soldiers led him away inside the palace (that is, the praetorium); and they called together the whole battalion. And they clothed him in a purple cloak, and plaiting a crown of thorns they put it on him. And they began to salute him, "Hail, King of the Jews!" And they struck his head with a reed, and spat upon him, and they knelt down in homage to him. And when they had mocked him, they stripped him of the purple cloak, and put his own clothes on him. And they led him out to crucify him.

Mark 15:16-20

Prayer

O God, I know that your Son, Jesus Christ, is King of heaven and earth; and yet, he allowed himself to be mocked and painfully crowned with a wreath of sharp thorns. His tormentors paid the homage that was truly due to him in a way that was a blasphemy before your holiness. He was stripped of all his human possessions, which completed the self emptying he had undertaken in his Incarnation. Help me to try to understand this total leaving behind of selfhood and divine power, Lord, for it is an awesome mystery which puts to shame my pretensions and my self pride. I pray for those who are mocked by a careless crowd because of their principles or beliefs and I ask that they will find courage in the example of Jesus. And I ask for guidance in my own life, Lord, so that I may know the right time to bow in true humility and the right time to stand and fight for the persecuted or for a righteous cause. Amen.

Themes for meditation

Those who are despised and rejected.
The responsibility that should go with power.
What is essential and what is non-essential in
   my life?
Finding my true centre with Christ.
Have I made any unjust decisions recently and
   how can I put them right?

Our Father . Hail Mary . Glory be to the Father

4. Carrying the cross

And as they led him away, they seized one Simon of Cyrene, who was coming in from the country, and laid on him the cross, to carry it behind Jesus. And there followed him a great multitude of the people, and of women who bewailed and lamented him. But Jesus turning to them said, "Daughters of Jerusalem, do not weep for me, but weep for yourselves and your children. For behold, the days are coming when they will say, 'Blessed are the barren, and the wombs that never bore, and the breasts that never gave suck!' Then they will begin to say to the mountains, 'Fall on us'; and to the hills, 'Cover us.' For if they do this when the wood is green, what will happen when it is dry?"

Luke 23:26-31

Prayer

O Lord, my God, I stand beside the road to Calvary and I watch you fall under the weight of the cross. I cannot stir to help you, Lord, for the weight of my sin roots me to the ground. I thank you for choosing Simon of Cyrene to help with that fearful cross, Lord, and I thank you that you are helping me to carry the weight of my cross through life. I praise you for inviting people who are heavily laden to come to you, and thankfully I come to you each day and lay my burden upon your shoulders. I pray for those who are burdened by guilt and yet cannot come to you for help because of ignorance or pride. I pray for prisoners who are waiting for death and ask that you will walk with them through the dark valley that leads to that other land beyond death's horizon. I know, Lord, because you have walked the road to Calvary, that there is a dawn beyond the grave, and I pray that you will abide with me from now until the hour when I meet the rising sun of resurrection. Amen.

Themes for meditation

Those who are alone and afraid.
That God will give me strength to help those
    weaker than myself.
Making each day a pilgrimage.
Those who are suffering from incurable illness
    or disease.
The meaning of repentance and turning to
    Christ.

◆

Our Father . Hail Mary . Glory be to the Father

5. The Crucifixion

*Now from the sixth hour there was darkness over all
the land until the ninth hour. And about the ninth
hour Jesus cried with a loud voice, "Eli, Eli, lama
sabachthani?" that is, "My God, my God, why hast
thou forsaken me?" And some of the bystanders hearing
it said, "This man is calling Elijah." And one of them
at once ran and took a sponge, filled it with vinegar,
and put it on a reed, and gave it to him to drink. But
the others said, "Wait, let us see whether Elijah will
come to save him." And Jesus cried again with a loud
voice and yielded up his spirit.*

Matthew 27:45-50

Prayer

O Lord, I kneel before the cross and I wonder at
the love you bear for all humankind. I ask myself
what kind of love can give so much with so
much pain and suffering, and I can only reply
that you, O God, were in that loving event, in
your Son, Jesus Christ. Your death on the cross,
Lord, was the most loving event ever to have
taken place on earth; and from that act of love,
more and more love has spilled into the world

from heaven. Each time the Eucharist re-enacts the giving of your body and blood, O Lord, your love again pours into the world and into the hearts of your faithful followers. This mystery is hard for me to understand, Lord, because the limits on my own love are limits also on my imagination. I pray for a portion of your self-giving love, that my heart may over-flow with love for those around me. I kneel before the cross and I wonder at your gracious love, Lord. Amen.

Themes for meditation

The love that encompasses all loves.
The pain that Christ endured.
Mary's grief at the cross.
The seven sayings of Jesus on the cross.
What the cross means to me.

Our Father . Hail Mary . Glory be to the Fat

THE FIFTH CHAPLET:

The Glorious Mysteries

1. The Resurrection

And when the sabbath was past, Mary Magdalene, and Mary the mother of James, and Salome, bought spices, so that they might go and anoint him. And very early on the first day of the week they went to the tomb when the sun had risen. And they were saying to one another, "Who will roll away the stone for us from the door of the tomb?" And looking up, they saw that the stone was rolled back – it was very large. And entering the tomb, they saw a young man sitting on the right side, dressed in a white robe; and they were amazed. And he said to them, "Do not be amazed; you seek Jesus of Nazareth, who was crucified. He has risen, he is not here; see the place where they laid him. But go, tell his disciples and Peter that he is going before you to Galilee; there you will see him, as he told you."

Mark 16:1-7

Prayer

O Lord, my God, how can I thank you for the glorious gift of the resurrection event to the world? I know that Christ has conquered death and sin, and I know that this gracious gift is freely given to everyone who has faith in him. In this universal act, Lord, you have conquered my sin and you have encompassed my resurrection. I pray for those who cannot believe in their salvation and I ask that their eyes may be opened to the saving work of Christ; for where there was despair, now there is hope; and where there was death, now there is life; and where there was defeat, now there is victory. I thank you for the symbols of resurrection which you have built into creation: the spring which follows winter and the seed which sprouts when a plant is dead; the dawn which follows the darkness of night and the waking which follows sleep. I thank you for the empty tomb and the good news of the resurrection given by the angel. Christ is risen! Alleluia! Amen.

Themes for meditation

New life in nature.
Eternity with Christ.
How can I be resurrected with Christ each day?
How an end can be a beginning.
Doors which providence has opened for me.

◆

Our Father . Hail Mary . Glory be to the Father

2. The Ascension

"But you shall receive power when the Holy Spirit has come upon you; and you shall be my witnesses in Jerusalem and in all Judea and Samaria and to the end of all the earth." And when he had said this, as they were looking on, he was lifted up, and a cloud took him out of their sight.

Acts of the Apostles 1:8-9

Prayer

O God, I thank you for the glorious mystery of the ascension of Christ into the dimension of heaven. I know that your creation in this earthly dimension is wonderful, Lord, and I can only imagine that the kingdom of heaven is even more wonderful. This further sign of glory to come lifts my heart and I praise you, Lord, with all my soul. I thank you for the last words of Christ to his disciples, especially for the command that they should be his witnesses throughout the world and throughout history. I thank you also for the glorious cloud of witnesses to the living Christ in the Church, and I pray that I may be a worthy witness to the

Gospel as I have met it in my life. I pray for an understanding of the relationship between earth and heaven. I give thanks for the Church both here on earth and in heaven, and I hope for the prayers of the saints for the continuing growth of the Church towards Christ. Amen.

Themes for meditation

People who have helped me in my faith.
What being a witness for Christ means.
The communion of saints
Christ the King in heaven.
How can I enrich the experience of worship?

◆

Our Father . Hail Mary . Glory be to the Father

3. The Descent of the Holy Spirit

When the day of Pentecost had come, they were all together in one place. And suddenly a sound came from heaven like the rush of a mighty wind, and it filled all the house where they were sitting. And there appeared to them tongues as of fire, distributed and resting on each one of them. And they were all filled with the Holy Spirit and began to speak in other tongues, as the Spirit gave them utterance.

Acts of the Apostles 2:1-4

Prayer

O God, Father, Son, and Holy Spirit, most glorious Trinity, I worship you and I praise you. I give thanks for the gifts of the Holy Spirit to the world and especially I thank you for the descent of the Spirit on the day of Pentecost. I pray, O Lord, that you will descend upon your Church with the power of wind and fire, that the body of Christians upon earth may be the body of Christ. Guide me, Lord, with your Holy Spirit, that I may walk in the way that I should go. Fill me with your Spirit of love that I may bring a little love to those around me. Give me the grace to use the gifts you have bestowed upon me for the good of the Church and for the benefit of my neighbour. O Lord, abide with me. In the name of the Father, and of the Son, and of the Holy Spirit. Amen.

Themes for meditation

Signs that the Holy Spirit is at work in the
    world.
The Holy Spirit working through the
    Scriptures.
The many gifts that people around me have
    been given.
The Gospel of the Holy Spirit as revealed in the
    Acts of the Apostles.
Messengers of the Holy Spirit.

Our Father . Hail Mary . Glory be to the Father

4. The Dormition/Assumption of the Blessed Virgin Mary

Lo! I tell you a mystery. We shall not all sleep, but we shall all be changed, in a moment, in the twinkling of an eye, at the last trumpet. For the trumpet will sound, and the dead will be raised imperishable, and we shall be changed. For this perishable nature must put on the imperishable, and this mortal nature must put on immortality.

1 Corinthians 15:51-53

Prayer

I thank you, O God, for the revelation that all the faithful will put on immortality like a garment when the timelessness of heaven repossesses the temporality of earth. I thank you for the gifts that the Blessed Virgin Mary has given to the world, especially in her example of obedience, humility and faithful love. I know, O Lord, that Mary resides in heaven with Christ and that she watches over the world, together with all the saints and angels, who intercede for us and protect your Church with the armour of their endless prayers. I thank you that the work of Mary continues and I pray that she will

mother the Church as she mothered the incarnate Jesus. I pray that the day will come
soon when heaven and earth will be fully one
realm and I ask that I may live daily in the light
of your kingdom until that day of the Lord
appears. Amen.

Themes for meditation

The perfect love which casts out all fear.
Mary in her many manifestations.
The joys and sorrows of parenthood.
God's ultimate aim for his creation.
The churches and organizations named after
    the Blessed Virgin Mary.

◆

Our Father . Hail Mary . Glory be to the Father

5. The Crowning of the Blessed Virgin Mary

Henceforth there is laid up for me the crown of righteousness, which the Lord, the righteous judge, will award to me on that day, and not only to me but also to all who have loved his appearing.

2 Timothy 4:8

Prayer

O Lord, my God, I give thanks for the crowning of Mary in heaven and for the crowning of all the martyrs and saints who have served you faithfully during their time on earth. I thank you for the patriarchs and apostles whom you called into your service and who answered the call without hesitation, and who now wear crowns before Christ the King. I pray that earthly rulers may have the wisdom that comes from heaven in carrying out their responsibilities to their peoples, so that they may deserve their earthly crowns. I pray also for the shepherds and rulers of the Church that they may rule for Christ and not for themselves. Before Christ in glory I bow my knee and I worship him, with

Mary and all the saints, with the whole Church and with all powers of heaven and earth. I ask, O Lord, that I may serve you to the best of my ability here upon earth and that I may join the joyful congregation of heaven when my service is completed. Amen.

Themes for meditation

The sovereign power of God.
The rulers of my own country.
The spiritual journey that lies ahead.
The temptation of Jesus to take earthly power,
    a policy he rejected.
The sick who will visit Lourdes this year.

Our Father . Hail Mary . Glory be to the Father

...heaven and all the smiles with the whole world... and within him between of Heaven and earth, I ask to Lord, that I may serve you in the rest of my ability that your goal, earth, and that I may fulfill... joyful congregation of Heaven when my service has completed. Amen...

...ruction...

The weapon power of God
The rulers of my own country, seem
The animals of a... that I act ahead,
The corruption of laws to... of this power,
a policy for aspect
The ... who will slay I sacrifice, this war

Our Lord... God that all may be to the Father,

THE SIXTH CHAPLET:

The Continuing Mysteries

1. The Saints

May you be strengthened with all power, according to his glorious might, for all endurance and patience with joy, giving thanks to the Father, who has qualified us to share in the inheritance of the saints in light.

Colossians 1:11-12

Prayer

O God, Father, Son, and Holy Spirit, I praise you and I thank you for all the saints, known and unknown, who have passed from earth to heaven. I am grateful that there are saints who in their earthly lives came from very ordinary backgrounds and who, in the strength of faith, put true humility before pride in their God-guided achievements. I thank you for those saints who showed the way to worship, for those who showed the way to love, for those who showed the way to deep spirituality, for those who saw visions sent from heaven and for those who showed the way to faithful service. I pray for those saints around me who go about their daily lives unnoticed, yet filled with faith, hope and love; and I pray for those who spend their gifts unstintingly for others, seeking no reward and uncaring about prestige or fame which may have come to them. I praise you and I thank you, Lord, for the example and inspiration of so many saints who have lived before me or with me. Amen.

Themes for meditation

A saint I admire.
What are the qualities of true saintliness?
One of the twelve apostles.
Women known to Jesus during his life on
    earth.
Saints of this century.

◆

Our Father . Hail Mary . Glory be to the Father

2. The Martyrs

Do not fear what you are about to suffer. Behold, the devil is about to throw some of you into prison, that you may be tested, and for ten days you will have tribulation. Be faithful unto death and I will give you the crown of life.

Revelation 2:10

Prayer

O Father of all, I thank you that men and women throughout the Christian centuries have been willing to give their lives as a witness to their faith in Christ. As Christ died and rose again, so have they died and risen again to join the mighty throng of the faithful in the kingdom of heaven. I know, Lord, that some have been tortured, or thrown to wild beasts, or raped, or starved, before they have been allowed to die. I pray for them a rich, new life in the company of Christ and for their tormentors the searching light of justice upon their evil deeds. I pray that I may have courage in my life, Lord, inspired by the example of the martyrs of the Church. I

thank you especially for the witness of St
Stephen, the first person known to have given
his life for Christ. For his vision and inspiration,
and for his forgiving words, I give praise and
thanks. Amen.

Themes for meditation

How to combat the destructiveness of violence.
The consolation of Christ's company through
   the storms of life.
The power of prayer.
Read Psalm 23 ["The Lord is my shepherd"]
   and allow the words to quieten the mind.
The loneliness of the victims of bullying or
   prejudice.

◆

Our Father . Hail Mary . Glory be to the Father

3. The Angels and Archangels

Bless the Lord, O you his angels, you mighty ones who do his word, hearkening to the voice of his word! Bless the Lord, all his hosts, his ministers that do his will! Bless the Lord, all his works, in all places of his dominion. Bless the Lord, O my soul!

Psalm 103:20-22

Prayer

O Lord of all dominions and powers, I praise you for revealing to your faithful people that you have created hosts of heavenly messengers to do your will. I thank you for the great archangels Gabriel, Michael and Raphael and for the pronouncements they have made to your servants. I thank you for the angels who were present with Christ throughout his earthly life. I thank you for all angels who guard us each day and night. I thank you for the guidance you give to your Church and for the word that comes to me in so many ways. I pray for the continuing guidance and guardianship of the angelic host, Lord, that the powers of evil in the world may never triumph. I pray for closer bonds between the heavenly and earthly realms through the mediation of your numberless angels, guided by your Holy Spirit. Hear my prayer, O Lord. Amen.

Themes for meditation

The invisible power for good that undergirds the universe.

How God uses people as well as angels to be his messengers.

Points in my life when I know God's angelic powers have been supporting me.

Infinity and eternity contrasted with space and time.

The blessing of a simple faith in God.

◆

Our Father . Hail Mary . Glory be to the Father

4. Christ the great High Priest in heaven

Since then we have a great high priest who has passed through the heavens, Jesus, the Son of God, let us hold fast our confession. For we have not a high priest who is unable to sympathise with our weaknesses, but one who in every respect has been tempted as we are, yet without sin. Let us then with confidence draw near to the throne of grace, that we may receive mercy and find grace to help in time of need.

Hebrews 4:14-16

Prayer

I praise you and I worship you, Lord of my life. I pray that you will show me daily how to love you and serve you more worthily, and how to bring to my worship a true spirit. I ask, O Lord, that our worship in the Church on earth may imitate the worship of the Church in heaven. I know, Lord, that Christ our High Priest is present with us as we worship and that he intercedes for the whole Church. I pray that our understanding of his leadership and our consciousness of his presence may grow, as we come to see that the congregation of heaven is also present with us as we worship; and that he is at the centre of all worship, drawing the faithful into the loving relationship of the Holy Trinity. Be in our worship, Lord, and fill your Church with the glorious light of heaven. Amen.

Themes for meditation

In what ways am I involved when I worship?
God's love is inseparable from his holiness.
Think about the words of a favourite hymn.
Think about the Lord's Prayer and its meaning.
Read the Creed thoughtfully.

◆

Our Father . Hail Mary . Glory be to the Father

5. The Second Coming

And while they were gazing into heaven as he went, behold, two men stood by them in white robes, and said, "Men of Galilee, why do you stand looking into heaven? This Jesus, who was taken up from you into heaven, will come in the same way as you saw him go into heaven."

Acts of the Apostles 1:10-11

Prayer

O God, come to me each morning as I awake, and stay with me each day as I work, and abide with me each night as I sleep. Help me to understand also, Lord, that through your Holy Spirit you are ever present in the Church as we celebrate the seasons and festivals from Advent to Advent. Yet you have promised that Christ will come again as a visible presence to claim his rightful kingdom and to rule the whole universe in an era of justice and of peace. I ask for a deeper understanding of this mystery among the faithful, Lord, and for a greater awareness of your presence in every corner of your creation, so that when the day of your coming is due your people may not be taken unawares. Maranatha! Come, Lord Jesus! Amen.

Themes for meditation

Am I ready today to meet Christ?
Jesus the Son of Man coming in glory.
The judgement of God.
The aim and purpose of human history.
The joy of knowing that Christ is with us.

◆

Our Father . *Hail Mary* . *Glory be to the Father*

Concluding Prayer

I praise you, Lord, that you called St Joseph to
be the foster father of your Son, Jesus Christ,
and I give thanks for the loving way
in which he performed his task.
I dedicate the completion of this rosary to him
and the Blessed Virgin Mary,
and pray that I may be moved
to follow their example,
and the example of all the saints,
in pursuing what is good and true in this life
and the next.
In the name of the Father, and of the Son,
and of the Holy Spirit. Amen

THE ROSARY

A book illustrating each Mystery of the Rosary and a quotation from the Gospel ending with a short reflection. Illustrations in full colour by Maurizio Boscolo.

◆

THE ROSARY

An attractive aid for saying the rosary. This pocket-size concertina booklet introduces the fifteen mysteries of the rosary with an appropriate biblical verse and a bible reading reference, followed by a very short prayer of petition. Each mystery is illustrated with a terracotta sculpture by Sr Angelica Ballan.